Family Walks
in Dorset

Nigel A. Vile

HIGH INTEREST LOW MILEAGE

Scarthin Books of Cromford
Derbyshire
1995

Family Walks Series

THE COUNTRY CODE

Guard against all risk of fire
Fasten all gates
Keep dogs under proper control
Keep to paths across farmland
Avoid damaging fences, hedges and walls
Leave no litter
Safeguard water supplies
Protect wildlife, plants and trees
Go carefully on country roads
Respect the life of the countryside

Published by Scarthin Books, Cromford, Derbyshire, 1995

Phototypesetting by Paragon Typesetters, Queensferry, Clwyd

Printed by Redwood Books

Maps by Ivan Sendall

Photographs by the author

Cover photograph: Shaftesbury by David Mitchell

ISBN 0 907758 86 X

Coast West of Durdle Door (Route 7)

Preface

Some of my first visits to Dorset were as a teacher, accompanying groups of youngsters on Geography fieldwork trips. Not being a Geography specialist, I would stand bewildered as youngsters were told to measure the various dimensions of no less than 150 pebbles at various points along Chesil Beach! The logic behind the exercise was lost on me, as I cast my eyes across a landscape that invited exploration rather than hypothesis testing.

Later visits were in the form of family holidays — to Swanage, Eype, Kimmeridge and Lyme Regis — when ranging poles, clinometers and metre rules could be left safely behind in the storeroom. This gave the opportunity to explore the rich varieties of landscape that the county has to offer the visitor — the rugged cliffs of Purbeck, the sheer spectacle of Chesil Beach, the crumbling coastline of West Dorset, the lonely Dorset Downs and the splendours of Cranborne Chase. Add to this the man-made features — vast hill forts, picture postcard villages, hill figures, delightful country inns and elements of industrial archaeology — and you have a county that only the most world-weary would find dull.

Dorset is without doubt one of the most beautiful of English counties. This collection of excursions provides the opportunity to sample a cross-section of its varied landscape types. From clifftop paths to downland tracks, from lofty hill fort sites to the settings of Thomas Hardy's novels, the county will surely hold out universal appeal. I hope that this volume of walks will provide you with many hours of enjoyment, as well as a host of happy memories.

Acknowledgements

Many thanks to my wife Gill for drawing the maps, and to my sister-in-law Trisha for the sketches that accompany some of the walks. My thanks also go to my own children — Laura, Katie and James — for being patient guinea-pigs on so many occasions!

About the Author

Nigel Vile teaches at King Edward's School in Bath. He was born in Bristol more years ago than he cares to remember, and currently lives in the Wiltshire town of Bradford-on-Avon. As well as this book of rambles, he is the author of several companion volumes that include the New Forest and Wiltshire. He is also a regular contributor to the Down Your Way section of Country Walking, Britain's leading walking magazine.

Contents

Map of the area

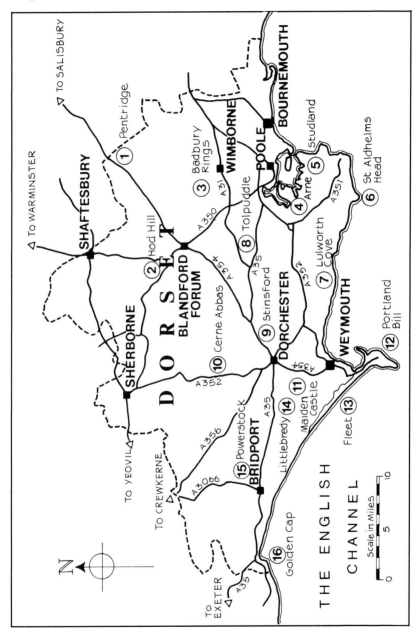

Map Key

➡➡➡➡	Route (footpath not always evident). All routes follow public rights of way	➡➡⬅	Section of route retraced on walk
– – – – – –	Footpath *not* on route	④ etc.	Number corresponding with route description
═══	Road	∿➡	Stream or river
+–+–+–+	Railway	▬▬	Canal
⬭	Lake or pond	⫽	Bridge
▪	Building	✚	Church
🌲🌳🌲	Wood	☀	Mound or hill
🏘	Town or village		

Curlew

7

Cranborne Chase

Outline
Pentridge − Peaked Post − Bokerley Dyke − Penbury Knoll − Pentridge

Summary
The Chase has been described as an 'open-air museum of archaeology' on account of its numerous ancient remains. These include a Bronze Age cursus, an Iron Age hill fort, one of Britain's best stretches of Roman road and Bokerley Dyke − an impressive Romano-British boundary. Cranborne Chase was also an historic royal hunting ground. Certainly, this 150,000 acres of open chalk grassland, woods and small coppices conveys a most regal presence to today's visitor. A fairly demanding family walk, that involves a couple of miles of high, exposed bridlepaths.

Attractions
Pentridge enjoys a secluded location, lying at the end of a lonely cul-de-sac lane. Its Celtic place-name literally translates as 'hill of the boars', testimony to the ancient origins of this settlement. The village featured as 'Trantridge' in Thomas Hardy's novel *Tess of the d'Urbervilles*. The literary connections continue in the village church, named after the 8th century Celtic Saint Rumbold. A tablet on the south wall of the nave commemorates Robert Browning, the first-known forefather of Robert Browning the poet. Their son Thomas, born in 1721, was the poet's great-grandfather. The poet, incidentally, always spoke of Pentridge as 'the cradle' of his family. If literary associations are of scant interest, look out for the kneelers and the choristers' cushions in St Rumbold's. These are hand-crafted with delightful rural designs − pheasants, cockerels, tractors, lambs, horses and even a trusty Land Rover!

A cursory glance at the O.S. sheets will show that Cranborne Chase is literally riddled with archaeological remains. One of the more spectacular relics on the Chase is Bokerley Dyke, an earth rampart of Roman-British origin. This 6-mile long line of defence, running between Blagdon Hill and the high ground that forms the northern part of Cranborne Chase, was constructed to protect the tribesmen of Dorset from Anglo-Saxon invasions. At one point, the dyke physically blocked the Roman road running from Dorchester to Old Sarum. Youngsters who find this historic detail somewhat dull can burn off excess energy recreating Anglo-Saxon forays into enemy territory.

Bordering Bokerley Dyke is Martin Down, a Nature Reserve jointly managed by Hampshire County Council and the Nature Conservancy Council. The reserve contains a number of fine downland habitats that include herb-rich turf, longer grassland, scrub, developing woodland and heath. Martin Down is renowned for its unusual species of butterfly, which include silver-painted skipper and Adonis blue. Ornithologists should also keep their eyes skinned for such feathered varieties as the nightingale, the hen harrier and the lesser whitethroat. W H Hudson wrote of Caleb

Bawcombe in his *A Shepherd's Life*. Caleb knew these downlands well, and commented:

> We must take what is sent. But if 'twas offered to me and
> I was told to choose my work, I'd say 'Give me my downs again
> and let me be a shepherd there all my life long'.

Refreshments
There are no pubs or cafes on this walk. The hilltops around Bokerley Ditch, however, offer many excellent picnic spots. The nearest pub is in the village of Sixpenny Handley, 3 miles west of Pentridge.

Public Transport
Wiltshire & Dorset Buses from Weymouth and Dorchester to Blandford Forum and Salisbury pass the Pentridge turning on the A354. Using public transport, the best option is to start the walk at point 2.

St. Rumbold's Church, Pentridge

9

Route 1

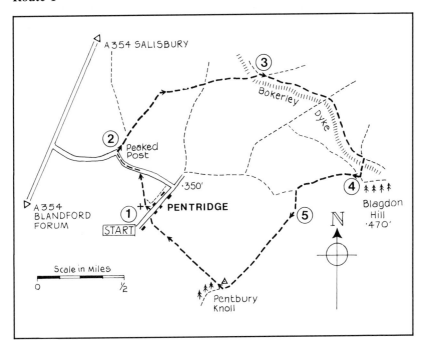

Cranborne Chase   4 miles

Start

Just south of the Hampshire-Dorset border, turn east off the A354 Salisbury to Blandford road along a lane signposted to Pentridge. Turn right into the village, and in a few hundred yards turn right on to an unmetalled lane signposted to the church and the village hall. There is limited parking available alongside the verges by these public amenities. GR 033179.

Route

1. *Cross the green opposite St Rumbold's Church to the top right-hand corner. Pass through the handgate, and follow the hedgerow to the left to the lane leading from the A354 to Pentridge. Turn left, and follow the lane for 300 yards until it bears sharply to the left at Peaked Post.*

2. *At this point, turn right off the road on to a bridlepath. Continue along this bridlepath for ¾ mile, ignoring one early left fork. In ¾ mile, another bridlepath crosses your path. Ignore this bridlepath, and continue straight ahead for ¼ mile until you reach a display board giving information about Martin Down Nature Reserve.*

3. *A few yards past the Nature Reserve sign, turn right to follow the path alongside Bokerley Ditch. Follow the Ditch for ¾ mile, Martin Down to the left, as the path gradually climbs towards Blagdon Hill. 100 yards from the hilltop, a chalk track cuts through the Ditch alongside another Nature Reserve sign.*

4. *Turn right along this track for 250 yards, then sharp right on to another track. In another 100 yards, turn left through a handgate and follow the enclosed path through the woods and out on to open ground. In a few hundred yards, the path enters an open field. Head half left across this field to a clump of trees in the far left-hand corner. Alongside these trees lies a gate and a horse jump.*

5. *Beyond the gate, follow the course of the hedgerow across the hilltop to Pentridge Knoll. This prominent hilltop is topped with a pine copse. Just as you enter this copse, turn right through the trees and follow the northern slopes of Pentridge Knoll back down towards Pentridge. Aim towards the tower of St Rumbold's. In the bottom left-hand corner of the field, cross a stile and continue along an enclosed path back into the village. Turn right at the road, and in a few yards left on to the track leading back to the church.*

Hod Hill and the River Stour

Outline
Stourpaine − Hod Hill − River Stour − Stourpaine

Summary
Hod Hill is the site of Dorset's largest Iron Age settlement, a site of some 54 acres that protected the important Stour Valley. The fort sits proudly atop a glorious chalk hilltop, with commanding views across the Stour. To escape the heavy hand of history, this walk also includes a delightful woodland path along the banks of the River Stour back to the village of Stourpaine. An easy walk that involves just one short climb on to Hod Hill itself. Be warned, however − the riverside path by the Stour can become very muddy during the winter!

Attractions
Any reference to Stourpaine in Dorset guidebooks talks at length about the nearby Hod Hill, with little mention of the village itself. In all fairness, it is a quite unremarkable settlement! Holy Trinity Church sits at the southern end of the main street, facing on to a large number of brick and flint cottages. Many of the houses carry the prefix 'Old' − the Old Schoolhouse and the Old Church House, for example − which speaks volumes about the decline of rural life in the past few years. Certainly, these one-time institutions make fine residences, but how much better village life must have been when these were active organisations and amenities.

On the edge of Stourpaine, our steps follow a footpath beside the River Iwerne. This tributary of the Stour is both clear and shallow, and will have youngsters positively crying out for a paddle. A towel should be a must in the old rucksack! Beyond the Iwerne, a delightful green lane climbs on to Hod Hill. The hedgerows that border this path are awash with flora in springtime − celandines, violets, catkins, primroses and bluebells all making a delightful picture. The many holes in the earth banks along the way also indicate the presence of foxes.

Hod Hill is the site of Dorset's largest Iron Age settlement, covering an area of some 54 acres. The Stour Valley was a route of strategic importance in centuries past, with the summit of this majestic chalk hilltop providing an unequalled vantage point. The site was not impregnable, however, falling to the 2nd Augusta Legion during the first few years of the Roman conquest. The Romans constructed a fort of their own in the north-western corner of the site, where as many as 700 men and 250 horses were garrisoned. Whilst nothing remains of the Roman occupancy, the fort's ramparts and ditches provide an excellent battleground for youngsters to burn off excess energy.

Refreshments

The White Horse Inn lies on the main A350 in Stourpaine. This hostelry is owned by Hall & Woodhouse, a local Blandford-based brewery. Hod Hill would make an excellent spot for a picnic.

Public Transport

Wiltshire & Dorset Buses run a Bournemouth to Blandford and Shaftesbury service that passes through Stourpaine.

Paddling in the Iwerne

Route 2

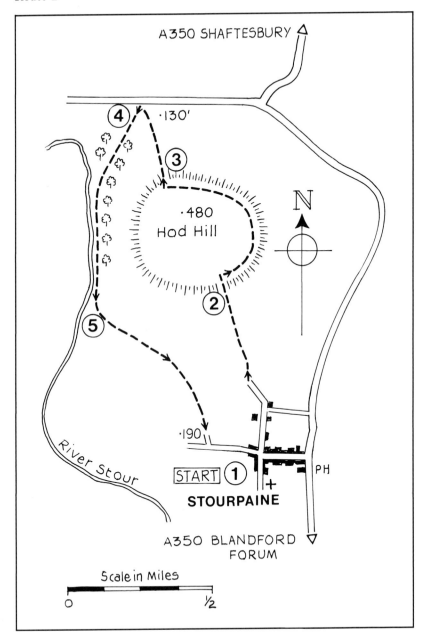

A350 SHAFTESBURY △

④ ·130'

③

·480
Hod Hill

N

⑤

②

·190

START ①
STOURPAINE

PH

A350 BLANDFORD ▽
FORUM

Scale in Miles

0   ½

River Stour

Route 2

Hod Hill and the River Stour   3 miles

Start

Stourpaine lies 3 miles north of Blandford Forum on the A350 Shaftesbury road. Turn into South Holme, alongside the White Horse Inn, and then left into Manor Road. At the end of Manor Road, park alongside Holy Trinity Church. GR 860094.

Route

1. *From the church, walk back along Manor Road, ignoring any left or right turns. In ¼ mile, the lane bears left to an isolated cottage. In another 75 yards, a signpost points the way along a bridlepath leading to Hod Hill. This path initially follows the banks of the Iwerne. before bearing left to climb uphill towards the summit of Hod Hill.*

2. *A stile and a National Trust sign bring you to the hill fort. Cross the stile, and climb up on to the ramparts on the right. Follow the path running along the top of the ramparts around the eastern and northern edges of the hilltop site. In the north-west corner of the hill fort, follow the track to the right that leads down to a stile and a National Trust information board.*

3. *Beyond this stile, follow the path ahead downhill across the field. It soon bears to the left to reach a gate/stile at the bottom of the field. Alongside the stile, a signpost reads 'Bridleway Hod Hill'. Beyond the stile, follow the path down through the woods and almost as far as the lane leading to Child Okeford.*

4. *Just before the lane, turn left and follow the bridlepath signposted to Stourpaine. This path soon borders the River Stour, whose riverbank is followed for close on ½ mile. The path subsequently bears to the left, and climbs away from the riverbank.*

5. *The enclosed path crosses open countryside as it heads back to Stourpaine. To the left, the southern ramparts of the hill fort dominate the skyline. Turn left at the first junction you reach in Stourpaine, and in a short distance you will find yourself back in Manor Road. A right turn returns you to Holy Trinity Church.*

Badbury Rings

Outline
Badbury Rings − The Beech Avenue − King Down Farm − Badbury Rings

Summary
Badbury Rings is an Iron Age hill fort protected by three concentric sets of ramparts and ditches. In a county renowned for its ancient relics, this must surely rank as one of the most impressive archaeological sites. The Rings border the Kingston Lacy Estate, where our steps follow a magnificent beech avenue. There is supposed to be a beech tree for every day of the year − now there's something to occupy the minds of restless youngsters! A very straightforward walk along generally level fieldpaths and bridleways.

Attractions
Badbury Rings represents one of the great Iron Age hill forts in Dorset. Situated on a chalk knoll, some 330 feet above sea level, the site commands views that stretch from the Purbeck Hills to Cranborne Chase. Three concentric sets of ramparts, the outer close on 1 mile in circumference, protect the hilltop enclosure. Legend maintains that this was Mount Badon, where King Arthur defeated the Saxons. An even more far-fetched tale suggests that King Arthur actually lived in the woods on the hilltop disguised as a raven! Whilst adults will prefer to sit and dwell on these historical details, youngsters can burn off excess energy re-enacting King Arthur's escapades against the invading Anglo-Saxons.

To the south-west of Badbury Rings lies Kingston Lacy Park, now in the hands of the National Trust. The centrepiece of the 16,000 acre estate is a 17th century country house, designed for Sir Ralph Bankes when his former home at Corfe Castle was damaged during the English Civil War. The walk passes through a magnificent avenue of beech trees, that runs from the gates of Kingston Lacy Park to what was formerly the edge of the estate. Tradition maintains that there are 365 trees running alongside one side of the avenue − one for each day of the year − with an extra tree on the opposite site to account for leap year. The beech is one of England's largest and most beautiful trees. It can reach a height of 100 feet in 100 years, whilst its girth continues to grow for many years after. The fruit − a 3-sided brown nut known as 'mast' − was once used extensively as pig-food. In some European countries, beech nut oil is still used as a substitute for butter.

The green lanes around Badbury Rings are awash with traditional English flora in the spring and summer months. Midsummer sees such varieties as knapweed and campion, scabious and bird's-foot trefoil bursting into flower. The bird's-foot trefoil takes its name from the arrangement of its seed pods. In some parts of the country, it is also known as 'bacon and eggs' due to the contrasting colour of the flowers and the buds. Be sure to take the 'I-Spy Wild Flowers' book on the walk, and youngsters will soon rise to the Honourable Rank of Botanist

Badbury Rings

17

Route 3

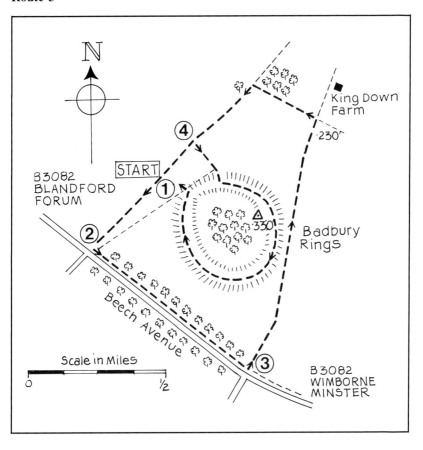

N

B3082
BLANDFORD
FORUM

START

King Down
Farm

·230·

Badbury
Rings

330

Beech Avenue

Scale in Miles

0   ½

B3082
WIMBORNE
MINSTER

Route 3

Badbury Rings   3 miles

Start

Badbury Rings lies alongside the B3082, midway between Blandford Forum and Wimborne Minster. Follow the signs to the NT car park alongside this ancient monument. GR 959030.

Route

1. *Pass through the kissing-gate that gives access to Badbury Rings from the car park. Turn right, away from the monument, and follow a track across the field back to the B3082.*

2. *Turn left at the main road, following the footpath alongside the road that passes beneath the magnificent avenue of beech trees. In nearly ¾ mile, opposite the turning to Sturminster Marshall, turn left on to a bridlepath.*

3. *Continue along this bridlepath for 1 mile, until you reach a cross-track just before King Down Farm. Turn left at this cross-track, and continue along another bridlepath for just ½ mile to a junction. Once again, turn left and follow another bridlepath back down to the NT land surrounding Badbury Rings.*

4. *Once you reach the grazing land that surrounds Badbury Rings, turn left across the field to reach the monument itself. Walk around the ramparts in a clockwise direction – approximately ¾ mile of walking – until the car park comes into view. Cut across the enclosure back to the parking area.*

Refreshments

There are no pubs or cafes on the route itself, although you should find an ice cream van in the car park at peak times. The open spaces around the car park provide many fine picnicking spots.

Public Transport

There is no bus service to Badbury Rings.

Salt Marsh alongside Poole Harbour

Arne and Arne Heath

Outline
Arne village − Shipstal Point − Shipstal Hill − Arne village

Summary
Arne is an isolated hamlet, 4 miles east of Wareham, that lies in the heart of a vast area of heathland bordering Poole Harbour. This unique habitat, home to both the Dartford warbler and the smooth snake, has rightly been accorded nature reserve status. As well as the rich flora and fauna, this walk also extends to Shipstal Point, site of a Roman salt-making complex. A large part of the walk follows an RSPB Nature Trail − permissive paths rather than rights of way − through level woodland and along coastal foreshore.

Attractions
The village of Arne lies on a large heath-covered peninsula that stretches northwards from the Isle of Purbeck into the heart of Poole Harbour. It is well worth spending a few minutes exploring the diminutive church before heading out to Shipstal Point. Although dating back to the 13th century, the building has been the subject of much alteration during the last century. All visitors to St Nicholas Church will be impressed by the view from the altar window, encompassing a large part of Poole Harbour.

The focus of interest on this walk is provided by the RSPB's *Shipstal Nature Trail*. Along the trail lies marshy woodland, saltmarsh, a sand spit, and crumbling cliffs. From the high point on the trail − Shipstal Hill − the many landmarks in the locality can be identified from a very useful topograph. The RSPB have produced a detailed leaflet to guide you around the trail. This is available at a modest charge from the car park, and should be a compulsory purchase!

On the fringes of Big Wood, overlooking Poole Harbour, lies a strategically placed RSPB hide. Don't forget to take a pair of field-glasses on this walk, and you may well be rewarded with sightings of cormorant, grey heron, curlew, oystercatcher, shelduck and redshank. The heron is a most fascinating bird to observe. It stands motionless besides shallow water, head sunk in its plumage or neck raised in an S-bend. If disturbed, the heron will take to the wing with a heavy flapping and legs trailing, uttering a 'kaark' of alarm.

Route 4

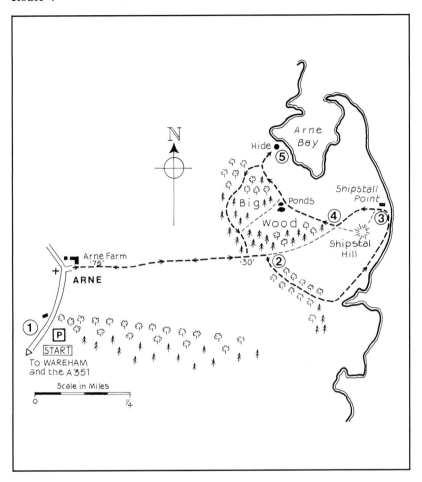

Route 4

Arne and Arne Heath   2 miles

Start

Head south out of Wareham, crossing the River Frome at South Bridge on the way to Swanage. In less than a mile, in the village of Stoborough, turn left on to the unclassified road leading to Arne. In 3 miles, as you enter Arne, park in the RSPB car park on the right-hand side. GR 973881.

Route

1. *Leave the car park and turn right along the road leading into Arne. The road passes Arne Toy Museum and St Nicholas Church, before bearing right and continuing as a bridlepath towards Shipstal Point. In just under ½ mile, the path passes a large RSPB display board on the right. This marks the start of the nature trail.*

2. *Leave the bridlepath, and turn right on to this trail. The well-used path initially passes through an area of woodland, before emerging alongside a saltmarsh on the fringes of Poole Harbour. A raised plank walkway takes the path down to a sandy beach, which is followed beneath crumbling cliffs around to Shipstal Point.*

3. *At the end of the beach, turn left on to a path that heads back inland. Where the garden wall on the right ends, leave the bridlepath and turn left on to a permissive path that climbs on to Shipstal Hill. This path climbs through bracken and gorse to reach the topograph on the hilltop. Follow the path behind the topograph back down to the bridlepath.*

4. *Cross the bridlepath, and follow the path opposite into an area of woodland. At the junction beyond a pair of ponds, continue on to the signposted hide. A right turn at the next junction brings you to the hide overlooking Poole Harbour.*

5. *Head back inland from the hide. Keep straight on along the path, ignoring all side turns, until you return to the bridlepath. Turn right, and retrace your steps along the bridlepath for ½ mile back to Arne.*

Refreshments

There is a picnic area in the RSPB car park in Arne. An equally attractive idea is to pack a picnic to enjoy on the beach overlooking Poole Harbour.

Public Transport

Arne is not served by public transport. A taxi from Wareham is the only option.

Studland and Old Harry

Outline

Studland – Ballard Down – Ballard Point – Old Harry – Studland

Summary

Studland offers visitors one of Britain's cleanest beaches, with excellent views that stretch across Poole Harbour to Bournemouth and beyond. The village is also the starting point for an excellent walk that explores Ballard Down, a chalk headland that looks across to the Needles and the Isle of Wight. At the furthest extremity of the headland stand a number of impressive chalk stacks, the most notable of which has earned the title of *Old Harry*. These fine natural features have become a popular nesting spot with cormorants and other sea birds. A quite strenuous walk, that involves one steep climb from Studland village high on to Ballard Down.

Attractions

The seaside village of Studland is a scattered mixture of old cottages, a few select hotels, a traditional inn and an historic church. St Nicholas is very much a Norman construction, a sturdy stone building with chancel, nave and low saddleback tower. Youngsters less interested in such architectural detail might prefer to seek out the corbel table that runs along the walls of the nave. The grotesque carved faces that adorn this feature will cause much amusement.

A large area of Ballard Down is now a National Trust property. This lofty headland is also a Site of Special Scientific Interest on account of its exceptional range of chalkland flora. Even the most reluctant of walkers will enjoy the views from the hilltop. To the south lies the seaside town of Swanage overlooking Swanage Bay, whilst northwards lies Studland Bay, Poole Harbour and Brownsea Island. Cast your gaze out to sea, and on a clear day the Needles at the western tip of the Isle of Wight are quite distinct.

The footpath along the eastern edge of Ballard Down runs above vertical chalk cliffs. Below lie a series of chalk stacks starting with *The Pinnacles* and ending up with *Old Harry* and *Old Harry's Wife*. The ledges that cling to these stacks and cliffs are noted nesting grounds for the cormorant. This large, long-necked, broad-winged seabird utters deep guttural grunts during the breeding season, which may explain those rather worrying noises you hear as you follow the cliff-top path! The cormorant swims low in the water, diving frequently in search of fish. It is an amusing occupation to guess where *Phalacrocorax Carbo* will resurface following a dive in search of food.

The beauty of a coastal walk is the 'bait' that can be held before reluctant youngsters . . . the prospect of a few hours on the beach at the end of the ramble. Studland Beach is indeed an enticing prospect. Three miles of fine sandy beach extend from the Sandbanks Ferry southwards to Old Harry. Better still, the beach has in recent years earned many accolades, including 'Cleanest Beach in England' in 1988.

Refreshments
The Bankes Arms lies at the end of the walk. This popular hostelry, with a fine reputation for its beers and food, welcomes family groups. A picnic could be enjoyed high on Ballard Down, or on Studland Beach at the end of the walk.

Public Transport
Wiltshire & Dorset Buses run a regular service between Bournemouth and Swanage that passes through Studland. Alight at the Studland Stores, and join the walk near Studland Church.

The Pinnacles

25

Route 5

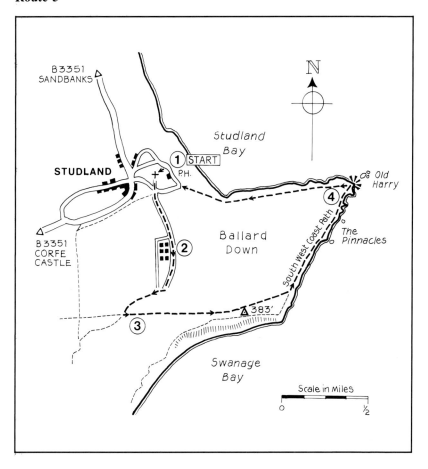

Route 5

Studland and Old Harry   4 miles

Start

Follow the B3351 from Corfe Castle through to Studland. Immediately before the Studland Stores, take the turning on the right signposted to the local church. In ¼ mile, this road bears sharply to the left and passes in front of the Bankes Arms. Park in the National Trust car park next to the inn (fee payable). GR 037825.

Route

1. *Leave the car park by the main entrance, turn left along the road and in just a few yards pass through a kissing gate on the left-hand side. Follow the enclosed path beyond this gate to St Nicholas Church. The path passes around the far side of the church and out into Church Road. At the end of Church Road, follow the bridlepath opposite alongside Manor Farmhouse. It is signposted to Swanage. In 250 yards, ignore a right turn and continue uphill alongside the left-hand edge of a rather select estate of houses.*

2. *Continue uphill, pausing to enjoy the views behind across Studland Bay. Beyond the last house, the lane bears to the right. At this point, pass through the handgate on the left to follow a footpath on to Ballard Down. The path climbs to the hilltop, where a conveniently placed stone bench bears the legend 'Rest and Be Thankful'. Pass through the gate alongside the beach, and turn sharp left to follow the hilltop fence towards the eastern extremity of Ballard Down.*

3. *The path continues along the top of the headland, stone marker posts pointing the way to Old Harry. Beyond the trig point − 385 feet above sea level − the path bears to the right, passes through a handgate and continues to the south-eastern tip of the headland. The path then bears northwards to run along the cliff edge towards Old Harry. EXERCISE EXTREME CAUTION WITH CHILDREN ALONG THIS UNFENCED CLIFFTOP PATH.*

4. *The path bears to the left alongside Old Harry to head back towards Studland. In close on 1 mile, having ignored any right turns, the path joins the lane in Studland alongside some public conveniences. Turn right to return to the Bankes Arms and the car park.*

St Aldhelm's Head

Outline

Worth Matravers − Winspit − St Aldhelm's Head − Chapman's Pool −
Worth Matravers

Summary

This walk explores perhaps the most dramatically rugged stretch of the Dorset coastline, praise indeed in a county with a plethora of natural coastal attractions. St Aldhelm's Head, 350 feet above the English Channel, is dominated by a Norman chapel whose turreted roof once supported a brazier. Its job was to warn sailors of the treacherous rocks at the foot of the cliffs. Along the way, the walk also passes through Winspit Bottom. The cliffs in the vicinity were the site of extensive quarrying, and contain easy-to-explore passages and tunnels. Naturally, local smugglers found these recesses of great value! This is perhaps the most demanding walk in the book for youngsters to tackle, although a short cut has been suggested to avoid the worst excesses of the coastal switchback.

Attractions

Worth Matravers is one of the prettiest villages on the Isle of Purbeck. Its original prosperity was built upon the local quarries, where Purbeck Stone was cut and hewn. The industry even lends its name to the village inn − the Square and Compass − a reference to the quarrymen's tools. The local buildings are all fashioned from Purbeck Stone, a grey, somewhat austere material. St Nicholas Church is worth exploring if for no other reason than to discover the grave of one Benjamin Jesty. This local man was a pioneer of cow vaccination, some 20 years before Edward Jenner. A memorable quote to Jesty runs: 'and who from his great strength of mind made the Experiment from the Cow on his Wife and two Sons'. Their reaction is not recorded!

Winspit is the site of a disused cliff quarry. Layers of stone were extracted, with vast Purbeck Stone pillars being left to support the roof. In places, the strata can be seen to be buckling under the weight. Should you be foolhardy enough to explore the old workings, you will literally take your life in your own hands! The stone was loaded directly into sea-barges for transhipment to Swanage, from where it was taken on to London. The quarries and caverns were also home to another local industry − smuggling. One notable local smuggler was Isaac Gulliver from nearby Worth Matravers. His generosity in sharing his spoil amongst the villagers made him a highly respected figure in the community. The quarrymen and the smugglers have long gone, leaving today's disused quarry as a nesting place for a large colony of bats.

St Aldhelm's Head stands some 350 feet above the sea. The Norman chapel just behind the headland is dedicated to the man who brought Christianity to the area in the 8th century, and who was later to become the first Saxon Bishop of Sherborne. The chapel is square in plan, with a turret at the apex of a pyramidal roof. This once supported a brazier, whose flames warned passing ships of the dangers that lurked around the headland. One vessel that did come to grief along this section of the Dorset coast was the East Indiaman 'Halsewell'. She was wrecked in 1786, with 168 members of her 250 strong crew being drowned. Many of the survivors were actually washed into the caverns at Winspit, where they lay until rescued by the local villagers. Incidentally, if you can make it to St Aldhelm's Chapel at dawn on Easter Day, you will be able to celebrate Holy Communion in one of the most picturesque settings in Britain.

Winspit Quarry

Route 6

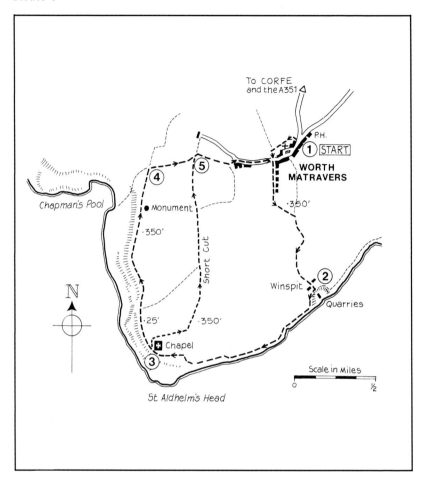

Route 6

St Aldhelm's Head   5 miles

Start

Leave the B3069 midway between Corfe Castle and Swanage to follow an unclassified road into Worth Matravers. There is a car park on the right as you enter the village. GR 974776.

Route

1. *Cross the stile in the corner of the car park, turn left and follow the edges of two fields around to St Nicholas Church. Walk around the church to the road, and turn right. In 200 yards, turn left along a lane signposted to Winspit. This lane eventually becomes a footpath which is followed towards the sea.*

2. *As you come within sight and sound of the sea at Winspit, turn right on to the Dorset Coast Path signposted to St Aldhelm's Head. Detour down to the sea if you wish to explore the old quarries. The path climbs above the quarry, and follows the coast around to the coastal look-out post high on St Aldhelm's Head.*
   NB: THIS UNFENCED PATH RUNS ALONG THE CLIFFTOPS – TAKE CARE!
   If your party is tired – or cannot face the prospect of a 350-foot descent and ascent – head inland past St Aldhelm's Chapel along a level track. This joins the road at Renscombe Farm, where you turn right to return to Worth Matravers.

3. *Having explored the area around St Aldhelm's Head – including the Norman chapel – continue along the coast path towards Chapman's Pool. In just 150 yards, there is a switchback as the path descends to sea level before climbing 350 feet back to the clifftops. The views are some consolation for the effort involved! Follow the path above the eastern side of Chapman's Pool until you reach a commemoration stone to the Royal Marines killed between 1945 and 1990.*

4. *In another 200 yards, look out for a stile in the wall on your right and a marker stone pointing the way to Renscombe. Cross this stile, and follow a well-worn path across a couple of fields that joins the track heading back from St Aldhelm's Head noted earlier. Cross this track, and follow the footpath opposite signposted to Worth.*

5. *This follows the left-hand side of a field across to Weston Farm. Turn left at the far side of this field to follow a track past some farm buildings and out on to the road. A right turn will return you to Worth Matravers and the car park.*

Refreshments

In Worth Matravers, you will find the Worth Tea Rooms and the Square and Compass Inn. St Aldhelm's Head would be an excellent spot for a picnic.

Public Transport

Wiltshire & Dorset Buses run a Poole to Swanage and Wareham service that occasionally passes through Worth Matravers.

St. Aldhelm's Chapel

Lulworth Cove and Durdle Door

Outline
Lulworth Cove − Durdle Door − Lulworth Cove

Summary
The coastline along the Isle of Purbeck truly deserves its heritage status. This spectacular walk explores two of the area's best known natural features. Lulworth Cove stands against a magnificent backdrop of vast chalk cliffs, whilst to the west lies Durdle Door. This vast natural arch has featured on many a postcard and calendar, and is responsible for keeping a number of local pleasure boats fully employed during the summer months! This dramatic coastal excursion will surely prove a highlight of any visit to Dorset. An easy coastal walk that includes a particularly dramatic section of the Dorset Coast Path.

Attractions
Lulworth Cove represents the classic oyster-shaped cove so beloved of geographers. The sea eroded a weak joint in the hard Portland limestone that lines the Dorset coast around Lulworth, enabling the waves to wear away the softer rocks that lay behind. The erosive power of the waves was only halted by a barrier of hard chalk, whose cliffs now form the backdrop to the Cove. Many yachts and small fishing vessels seek shelter in Lulworth Cove, continuing a long seafaring tradition. In the 18th and 19th centuries, smugglers brought their contraband ashore in this sheltered spot, with the barrels of liquor being hidden in nearby caves.

Alongside Lulworth Cove lies Stair Hole. This is a cove in the very process of formation. Once again, the sea has breached the hard Portland limestone and is slowly eroding the softer rocks further inland. Eventually, the destructive power of the waves will wear away the rocks separating Stair Hole from Lulworth Cove, forming one vast sheltered inlet from the sea.

Durdle Door is a vast rock arch, formed from near vertical beds of Portland stone that are joined to the mainland by Wealden clays. Arches evolve over time − waves initially wear away a joint in the rock to form a small cave. Wave action gradually attacks this small cave, eroding through the rock until the arch is formed. Either side of Durdle Door lie fine beaches. It is well worth climbing down the steps to one or other of these beaches as a halfway break on this walk. If you intend doing this, however, don't forget to pack towels and beach gear to avoid the wrath of youngsters in your party!

Route 7

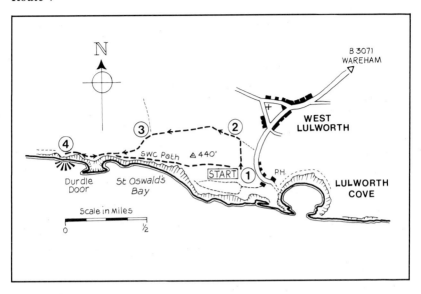

Durdle Door

Lulworth Cove and Durdle Door   2 miles

Start

Follow the B3070 from Wareham to Lulworth Cove, where you will find a large car park on the right as you enter the village − GR 821801. Alternatively, follow the B3071 southwards from Wool to Lulworth Cove.

Route

1. *Walk to the far side of the car park, where a stile gives access to the steep hillside path leading to Durdle Door. Once across this stile, turn sharp right along a path signposted 'Coast Path Youth Hostel'. DO NOT follow the more obvious path ahead signposted to Durdle Door. Our path follows the fence on the right for ¼ mile to a second stile.*

2. *Continue following the fence, along the footpath signposted 'Durdle Door Campsite'. This path continues for ½ mile across several fields, always running alongside the field boundary on the right. The path eventually emerges on to a rough track alongside a caravan site.*

3. *Turn left, taking the path signposted to Durdle Door. The path passes through a parking area before starting its steep descent down the hillside. The right of way soon bears to the right to reach Durdle Door.*

4. *Having enjoyed the magnificent coastal scenery around the fine natural arch, head back along the path followed down from the caravan site. In a short distance, however, do not bear left to return to the campsite. Rather, follow the path that clings to the coast signposted to Lulworth Cove. This path climbs the hillside before dropping steeply back into the Lulworth Cove parking area.*

Refreshments

There are several pubs, cafes, tea shops and restaurants in Lulworth Cove.

Public Transport

Occasional bus services operate from Weymouth and Wool to West Lulworth and Lulworth Cove. These services are operated by Garrison Cars of Wool.

Lulworth Cove

Tolpuddle and Weatherby Castle

Outline

Tolpuddle — Ashley Barn — Weatherby Castle — Tolpuddle

Summary

Tolpuddle is an attractive village, lying alongside the somewhat infamous River Piddle! The manor and the 13th century stone and flint church will catch the eye of the historian, as will the many associations in the village with the Tolpuddle Martyrs. To the north of Tolpuddle, high on the Dorset hills, lies Weatherby Castle. This Iron Age settlement contains an interesting brick obelisk, erected in 1761. The hilltop site is covered with trees, which adds to its shrouded and mysterious appeal. This is one of the longer walks in the book, although the fieldpaths and bridleways that are followed cross relatively gentley countryside. A picnic half-way round the circuit at Weatherby Castle would provide a suitable rest break.

Attractions

Tolpuddle is one English village whose fame stretches far beyond Albion's shores. It was here during the first half of the 19th century that 'six men of Dorset' used to meet and discuss how the lot of the local agricultural workers could be improved. Their crime was not that they sought to form a trade union, rather it was the part each played in 'the administration of an illegal oath'. In 1834, the six Tolpuddle Martyrs were sentenced to transportation to Australia following their trial at Dorchester Crown Court. Following a vigorous campaign in the months that followed, the Tolpuddle Martyrs were shipped back to England in 1836. Only James Hammett returned to the village of his birth, and his mortal remains now lie buried in the local churchyard. The tombstone reads:

James Hammett

Tolpuddle Martyr

Pioneer of Trades Unionism

Champion of Freedom

Born 11 December 1811

Died 21 November 1891

Other reminders of the Tolpuddle Martyrs lie scattered around the village. The TUC Memorial Cottages each bear the name of one of the martyrs, with a central hallway housing a museum devoted to this dark episode in English history. On *The Green* stands the Martyrs' Seat and Shelter, commemorating the spot where the farm labourers used to meet under a sycamore tree to discuss their common concerns. The Methodist Chapel houses a memorial arch to the martyrs, whilst Thomas Stanfield's Cottage — another meeting place — still stands alongside the Dorchester Road. A village guide, detailing these places of interest, can be purchased in St John's Church

Continued on page 40

Route 8

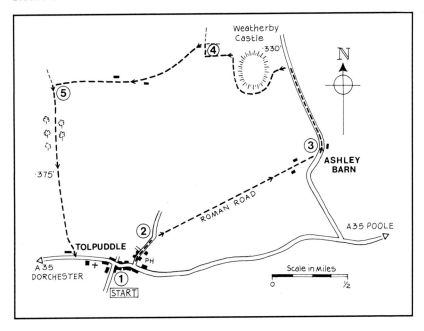

Route 8

Tolpuddle and Weatherby Castle   5 miles

Start

*Tolpuddle lies 8 miles east of Dorchester, on the A35 Bournemouth trunk road.
As you approach the centre of the village from the west, turn right into 'The Green'
and park alongside the Martyrs' Shelter. GR 792944.*

Route

1. *Return to the busy A35, turn right and walk almost as far as the Martyrs Inn. Just
   before this hostelry, turn left into Whitehill. Climb up the hill and, just before the
   road reaches the hilltop, turn right through a gateway on to a bridleway marked
   by an overgrown signpost. The legend actually reads 'Ashley Barn'.*

2. *The bridlepath crosses a field to a pair of gates, a fine view of the Piddle Valley
   to the south. Pass through the left-hand gateway and follow the hedgerow on your
   right through the next two fields. In the corner of the second field, the bridlepath
   passes through a handgate into an oak spinney. Continue through this spinney, and
   follow the left-hand boundary in the next field on to an enclosed track. This track
   passes through a farmyard before emerging on to the lane in Ashley Barn.*

3. *Turn left and follow this lane for ½ mile. As it passes beneath the wooded slopes
   of Weatherby Castle, look out for a metal stile in the hedgerow on the left. Cross
   this stile and follow an ill-defined fieldpath around the southern and western edges
   of Weatherby Castle. As you pass alongside the western side of Weatherby Castle,
   look out for a fence/hedgerow in front of you at the far side of the field. Follow
   this downhill to the left, to a stile in the bottom corner of the field. Once across
   this stile, cross a second stile on the right and follow the fieldpath alongside the
   hedgerow out on to a bridlepath.*

4. *Turn left, cross a stream and follow the track past a row of beech trees to a
   gateway. Cross the next field towards a barn, to the right of which an enclosed
   path runs along the valley bottom to a handgate. The path continues along the
   bottom of the valley beyond this gate to another gateway. Cross the next two fields,
   keeping the hedgerow to your right, until you come to a gap in the hedge in the
   far corner of the second field. En route, you will pass a complex of old farm
   buildings, as well as crossing a track.*

5. *Once through this gap, turn left along an enclosed path. This path climbs to the
   hilltop, where it enters an open field with fine views opening up. Follow the left-
   hand boundary through the first two fields, and aim for the far left-hand corner
   of the third field where an enclosed path heads back down into Tolpuddle. This*

track continues down to the A35, where a left turn will bring you back to 'The Green' in the middle of the village.

Refreshments
In Tolpuddle, the Martyrs Inn lies on the main A35 just east of *The Green*. A picnic could be enjoyed on the slopes of Weatherby Castle.

Public Transport
Wiltshire & Dorset Buses running between Dorchester and Poole pass through Tolpuddle.

The Martyrs Shelter, Tolpuddle

Continued from page 37
in Tolpuddle.

Beyond Tolpuddle, the walk passes through the fertile Dorset countryside. This is a landscape dominated by mixed farms, where fields of wheat, barley and maize lie alongside sheep pastures and grazing cattle. In the hamlet of Ashley Barn, the footpath literally passes through the middle of a farmyard, surrounded by barns, farm machinery, cowsheds and a milking parlour. Youngsters equipped with the *I-Spy On the Farm* book will have plenty to keep them occupied throughout this walk. By journey's end, it should be possible to have accumulated enough points to reach the 'Honourable Rank of Farm Spy'.

Weatherby Castle marks the site of an Iron Age settlement. In a county with many excellent ancient monuments, Weatherby tends to get overlooked by the guide-book writers. The ramparts surround a wooded hilltop, a fine area for youngsters to explore and release excess energy. In the woodland stands an unusual brick obelisk erected in 1782 by a former landowner. His identity is now long forgotten, since the memorial tablet has disappeared! Some experts believe that the monument was the inspiration behind Thomas Hardy's *Two on a Tower*, written between 1881 and 1883 when Hardy was living in Wimborne.

Puddletown Forest and Hardy's Cottage

Outline
Higher Bockhampton − Stinsford − Lower Bockhampton − Thorncombe Wood − Hardy's Cottage − Higher Bockhampton

Summary
A delightful walk into the heart of Hardy country. This is the landscape of Hardy's youth, where he gained inspiration for such fine novels as *Under the Greenwood Tree* and *Far From the Madding Crowd*. Amidst the villages, churches and trees that inspired his writings, our steps fall upon the beautiful thatched cottage where Hardy himself was born in 1840. A delightful literary trail that follows gentle fieldpaths, quiet riverside footpaths and a woodland trail.

Attractions
Thomas Hardy (1840-1928) was one of England's finest novelists and poets. His writing was inspired by the Wessex landscape in general, and the Dorset countryside in particular, which acts as an ever-present backdrop to his novels. An architect by training, his first literary success came in 1874 with the publication of *Far From the Madding Crowd*. Hardy's work has been described by one critic most succinctly:

> '. . . remarkable for the background contrast of richly humorous rustic characters, for the brooding intensity of human loves and hates played out before the harshly indifferent force of the natural world'.

Hardy's Cottage, a small two-storey thatched dwelling, was where the great novelist was born on 2 June 1840. The cottage was built in 1800 by his great-grandfather, and remained the family home for several generations. Hardy's grandfather was involved in a small way with brandy smuggling, and added a narrow opening in the porch to keep his eye open for the excisemen! Hardy himself was born in the middle bedroom, where he later worked at his desk on titles such as *Far From the Madding Crowd* and *Under the Greenwood Tree*. The last word on the cottage should be left to Thomas Hardy:

> 'It faces west, and round the back and sides high beeches, bending, hang a veil of boughs, and sweep against the roof'.

Stinsford was the 'Mellstock' featured in *Under the Greenwood Tree*. St Michael's Church, with its 13th century arcades, square Norman font and Saxon relief of St Michael with spread wings, is the resting place of the Hardy family's mortal remains. Hardy's parents, his sister and his first wife Emma are all buried in the churchyard, together with Thomas Hardy's heart . . . his remaining ashes were buried in Poet's Corner at Westminster Abbey. Cecil Day Lewis, the Poet Laureate, is also buried at

St Michael's Church. His tombstone records the following verse:

> Shall I be long gone
> For ever and a day?
> To whom there belong?
> Ask the stone to say.
> Ask my song.

Thorncombe Wood and Black Heath Trails are a 66-acre nature reserve bordering the western fringes of Puddletown Forest. The area is owned and administered by Dorset County Council, who publish an informative leaflet describing the nature trail (available at the car park). The leaflet describes the flora and fauna in some detail. Suffice it to say that this will be a paradise for youngsters interested in natural history. Oaks, silver birch, larch and chestnut trees provide fine cover for jays, treecreepers, nuthatches and woodpeckers. Mammals, including squirrels, foxes, deer and badgers also make their homes in Thorncombe Wood, where the speckled wood butterfly is a summer resident, too.

The Hardy Family Grave

42

Thomas Hardy's Cottage

43

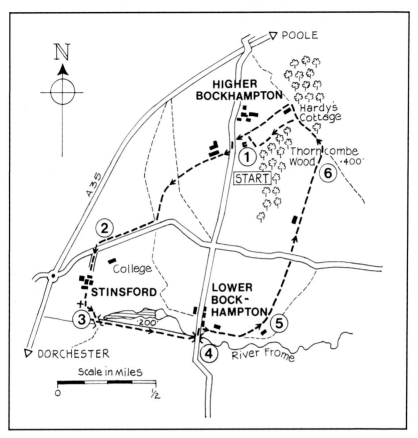

Fly Agaric

44

Puddletown Forest and Hardy's Cottage   4 miles

Start

As the A35 approaches Dorchester from Puddletown, turn left on to an unclassified road leading to Higher Bockhampton. As you enter this scattered settlement, turn left along the signposted lane leading to Hardy's Cottage. A car park is provided for visitors to both the cottage and the Thorncombe Wood Nature Trail. GR 726922.

Route

1. *Walk back to the road, and turn left. In a short distance, follow the bridlepath on the right signposted to Stinsford. This enclosed path ends by a barn, where you pass through the handgate directly ahead and follow the hedgerow beyond to a second gate. Cross the field ahead to a gate in the bottom corner, and the lane leading to Stinsford and Dorchester.*

2. *Just before the lane, bear right to follow a footpath signposted to Stinsford. This path runs through a small enclosure, parallel to the road itself, saving a stretch of road walking. The path emerges on to the road by a signpost pointing the way back to Higher Bockhampton. Turn right at the road and, in 200 yards, left along the lane signposted to Stinsford Church. The lane passes alongside part of the Dorset College of Agriculture before reaching St Michael's.*

3. *Enter the churchyard, and follow the path to the right that passes the church door before going around to the back of the church. Leave the churchyard by a wooden handgate, and follow the path to the right down to a cross-track just beyond a stream. Turn left, following the gravelled track signposted to Lower Bockhampton. Watercourses line both sides of this delightful footpath.*

4. *The path emerges on to a lane. Turn left, cross the river, and walk as far as a thatched cottage on the right — Bridge Cottage. Turn right at this point, following a path signposted to Thorncombe Wood. The path soon passes through a farmyard before entering an open field. Cross to a stile alongside a patch of woodland, 150 yards ahead, and aim for a gate in the top left-hand corner of the next field.*

5. *Beyond this gate, follow the track to the left signposted (again) to Thorncombe Wood. When this path reaches the Stinsford to Tincleton road, cross over and follow the track opposite leading to Pine Lodge Farm. This path passes to the right of the farm buildings, before entering an open field. Follow the left-hand side of this field to a gate in the corner where the path enters Puddletown Forest.*

6. *Follow the path on the right, past the firebeaters, and on through holly trees for 200 yards until you glimpse a pond through the bushes on the left. Just past the pond, follow the path on the left signposted to Hardy's Cottage. The well-defined woodland path leads down to the birthplace of Dorset's best-known writer. To return to the car park, retrace your steps to the back of the cottage. Rather than returning along the left-hand path to the pond, fork right along a path that heads back through the trees to the parking area. En route, you meet one cross-track, where you turn right.*

Refreshments
There is a picnic area alongside the car park. Commercial refreshment facilities abound in the nearby town of Dorchester, where the Tourist Information Centre carries a vast selection of literature on Thomas Hardy.

Public Transport
Wiltshire & Dorset Buses running from Dorchester to Poole all pass the Higher Bockhampton turning alongside the A35.

Stinsford Church

46

The Cerne Abbas Giant

Outline
Cerne Abbas — Giant Hill — The Giant — Cerne Abbas

Summary
Cerne Abbas, nestling deep in the Cerne Valley, is a beautiful stone, brick and flint village that must surely rank as one of the most handsome settlements in all of Dorset. To the north of Cerne Abbas rises Giant Hill, on whose slopes is carved a massive 180-foot long hill figure ... who is not afraid to display his modesty! Beyond the Giant lies an ancient earthwork — known as the 'Trendle' — that was the site of ancient May Day rituals until recent times. An intriguing walk across the mysterious Wessex landscape, with just one strenuous climb up the steep slopes of Giant Hill.

Attractions
Dominating the hillside above Cerne Abbas is the infamous Cerne Abbas Giant. This 180-foot high figure of a naked male is thought to be the work of the Romano-British. The figure was allegedly based upon the Roman Emperor Hercules, who claimed to be an incarnation of Heracles. Heracles was a fertility god, which explains the somewhat lewd nature of the hill figure. Whether or not the giant should feature in a book of family walks is perhaps debatable! If talk of ancient history leaves you cold, perhaps the local legend of the giant's origin will hold more appeal. The story goes that at one time a giant was responsible for eating the villagers' sheep. The local shepherds took the law into their own hands and slaughtered the evil piece of work. As a reminder to other would-be attackers, the victim of their recriminations was carved on the hillside ... in a most immodest manner!

Above the giant lies an earthwork known as the 'Trendle'. This was the site of pagan ceremonies, where a maypole was erected on May Day until quite recent times. The maypole originated as a fertility symbol in pagan times, with the pole regarded as a phallus. That the ceremonies should take place alongside the giant comes as no surprise, with the hill figure proudly displaying his 30-foot long specimen! Due to the pressure of visitor numbers, the National Trust have fenced off both the giant and the neighbouring earthwork. Visitors can best view the giant from Giant View, on the A352 just to the north of Cerne Abbas.

The village of Cerne Abbas has a long and illustrious history. A Benedictine abbey was founded here in the 10th century, the remains of which can be seen towards the end of the walk in the field before the church. St Mary's Church is worth visiting to see its 15th century rood screen, the Jacobean pulpit with its canopy or 'tester' and the 14th century wall paintings in the chancel. If ecclesiastical architecture is lost on your youngsters, then leave them in the stocks that lie in the street outside the church! In the 18th century, a large brewing industry was established in the village to supply

Continued on page 50

Route 10

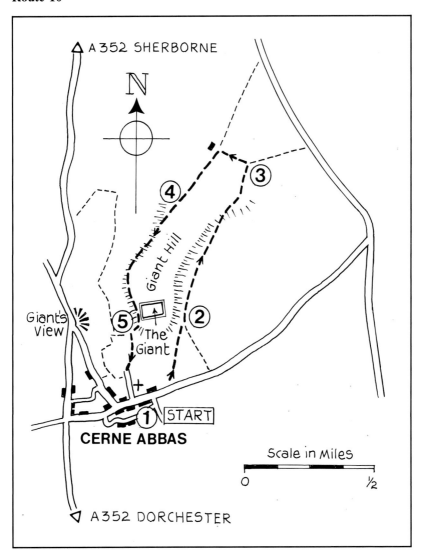

Route 10

The Cerne Abbas Giant 2½ miles

Start

Cerne Abbas lies 8 miles north of Dorchester, on the A352 Sherborne Road. Park in the main street through the village — Long Street — somewhere in the vicinity of St Mary's Church. GR 665012.

Route

1. *Continue along Long Street in an easterly direction until, 200 yards outside of Cerne Abbas, an unmarked bridlepath turns off on the left-hand side. This is immediately past the entrance to the local sports ground. Follow this bridlepath to a gateway.*

2. *Beyond this gateway, the path soon bears to the right and climbs the steep eastern slopes of Giant Hill. Far-ranging views across Yelcombe Bottom soon open up. At the top of the hill, follow the fence ahead for 200 yards to a gate on your left.*

3. *Pass through this gateway, and head across a field following the fence on your right. Halfway across, you will come to a barn on the right-hand side. At this point, turn left and follow an ill-defined fieldpath across the hilltop. This right of way bears to the right to cross a stile in the right-hand field boundary, almost at the far side of the field.*

4. *Beyond the stile, the path bears to the left and begins its descent of Giant Hill. Eventually, the path passes beneath the boundary fence of the Giant's enclosure into a small area of woodland.*

5. *Turn right almost as soon as you enter the trees, and look out for a stile on the left-hand side. Cross this stile, and head across the field beyond to Cerne Abbas churchyard. Beyond the churchyard, continue down the lane past St Mary's Church and back into Long Street.*

Refreshments

There are pubs and tea rooms in Cerne Abbas, including the Royal Oak and the Red Lion, which both feature in *The Good Pub Guide*. Giant Hill, with its many vantage points, would be an excellent spot for a picnic.

Public Transport

Wiltshire & Dorset Buses operating between Dorchester and Sherborne pass through Cerne Abbas.

Continued from page 47

fine ales to London hostelries. This explains the presence of several exceptional inns in the village today.

Royal Oak Inn, Cerne Abbas

Maiden Castle

Outline
A circular perambulation of Maiden Castle.

Summary
Thomas Hardy was certainly impressed with this vast hill fort just a mile or so outside Dorchester. His description of what is widely held to be one of Europe's most impressive ancient monuments was certainly eloquent: 'It may be likened to an enormous, many-limbed organism of an antediluvian time, lying lifeless, and covered with a thin green cloth, which hides its substance, while revealing its contour'. A hilltop walk across a deserted landscape that once positively hummed with the sound of human activity. Be sure to pick a fine, clear day, the hill fort site being particularly open and exposed.

Attractions
Maiden Castle sits proudly on top of a vast chalk hilltop, just 1 mile south-west of Dorchester. From its lofty vantage point, it is easy to see why generations of settlers have targetted this strategic site as the prime location in the area.

As early as 3,500 BC, a Neolithic camp occupied the hilltop. By 350 BC, Iron Age settlers had made Maiden Castle their home. The hilltop would have been covered with timber huts, surrounded by vast defences broken only by well-guarded gateways. Archaeologists estimate that as many as 5,000 people occupied the site, tilling the surrounding fields and tending their sheep and cattle.

In AD 45, Vespasian's Second Legion stormed the fortress and the hilltop fell into the hands of the Romans. The fighting was fierce, with the Romans facing an onslaught of sling stones — round pebbles gathered from Chesil Beach. The Second Legion won the day, however, and countless bodies were buried in a graveyard near the eastern entrance to the fort. Many of the skeletal remains have been unearthed by archaeologists and are on display in Dorchester's excellent County Museum. On the site itself, the foundations of a Roman temple remain to this day.

Place-names help us to interpret our surroundings. Maiden Castle, for example, is thought to derive from 'Mai Dun'. The experts, however, disagree on the meaning of this phrase. It could mean 'flat-topped hill' or 'the settlement on a hill' according to some. I prefer the more down-to-earth rendering of 'the great mound'. Whatever translation is correct, the descriptions certainly add to our understanding of the landscape. As we follow the lane beneath the southern slopes of Maiden Castle, the South Winterborne runs in the neighbouring fields. Here, too, is an interesting place-name. Knowing that a 'borne' is a small stream, you should be able to work out the rest for yourself. This might explain why in high summer the South Winterborne is nothing more than a shallow ditch!

Route 11

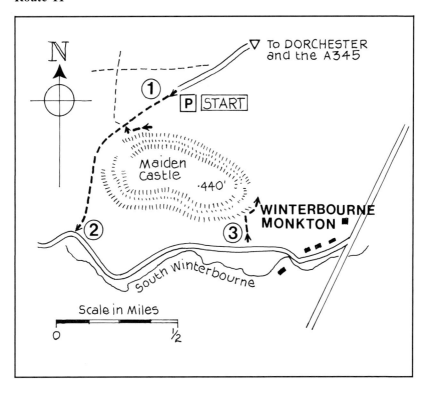

Route 11

Maiden Castle   2½ miles

Start

As you leave Dorchester town centre on the A354 Weymouth road, an unclassified road on the right-hand side is signposted to Maiden Castle. This cul-de-sac lane ends at the site's car park. GR 669889.

Route

1. *Follow the well-worn chalk path leading uphill to the monument. At the top of the climb, pass through a handgate on the right-hand side. Immediately past this gateway, turn left to follow a bridlepath that skirts the western ramparts of the fort. This enclosed path ends at an open field, where you continue down through the dip to the Martinstown to Winterborne Monkton lane.*

2. *Turn left, and follow this quiet lane as it runs in the shadow of the giant hill fort. In close on 1 mile, look out for a handgate on the left-hand side of the road. Beyond this handgate, follow the fieldpath up the hillside. It runs alongside a hedge to the south-eastern corner of Maiden Castle. Pause at the kissing-gate giving access to the hill fort site to enjoy the view back across the valley carrying the South Winterborne.*

3. *Enter the hilltop site, and follow the ramparts on the right. These will take you around the eastern and northern sides of the fort. You emerge by the main entrance to the hill fort, where the path leads back to the car park. NB: This is the quickest route back to the car park. I recommend that you deviate from this route to explore the hilltop site more carefully − otherwise you will miss the remains of the Roman temple.*

Refreshments

Pubs and cafes in Dorchester, just 1 mile from the start of the walk.

Public Transport

No buses run to the site, which is only a short taxi ride from the centre of Dorchester. Dorchester is well served by bus and rail services.

Around Portland Bill

Outline

Portland Bill − Wallsend Cove − East Cliffs − Portland Bill

Summary

The Isle of Portland is in fact a peninsula, linked to the mainland by a long strip of shingle known as Chesil Beach. Portland Bill is the southern tip of this peninsula, and is the site of rugged limestone cliffs, a pair of lighthouses and a number of small caves. 'The Bill' is also a magnet for large numbers of seabirds. A wild and exciting excursion, that follows generally level coastal paths that enjoy quite exceptional views.

Attractions

Thomas Hardy made frequent references to Portland in his novels. In *The Well Beloved*, he named it 'the Isle of Slingers' − no doubt a reference to a skill possessed by the islanders in ancient times. Hardy also described Portland as 'the Gibraltar of Wessex'. This is no real island, however, being a vast slab of grey rock linked to the mainland by Chesil Beach. The actual dimensions of Portland are 4 miles from north to south, and up to 2 miles wide. The island slopes from the high ground of the Verne in the north, rising to over 500 feet, down to the shallow cliffs of Portland Bill in the south. After the walk around Portland Bill, it is worth seeking out Portland Castle and Portland Museum, both excellent attractions for visitors, where you will learn a lot more about the history and traditions of this unique corner of Dorset.

Portland Bill is the name given to the rocky southern tip of the island. The Bill is dominated by a colourful 136-foot high lighthouse, which even manages to eclipse the massive stack at the island's extremity known as 'The Pulpit'. Portland Bill has always been something of a ship's graveyard, so it comes as no surprise to discover George I issuing a patent for a lighthouse to be constructed hereabouts in 1716. The original pair of lighthouses contained enclosed lanterns and coal fires to warn passing ships of the dangers lurking around the Bill. Today's lighthouse was established in 1906. The light has an intensity of 674,000 candela, and a range of 25 sea miles. Visitors willing to negotiate 153 steps can ascend the tower to secure perhaps the best views on Portland.

Portland has always been well-known for its stone. From St Paul's Cathedral to the United Nations Building in New York, uses have always been found for Portland Stone. Although working dates back to the Middle Ages, it is only since the 17th century that extensive quarrying has occurred on Portland. The peak year for working was 1899, when 1,441 men were employed in over 50 quarries. Due to the shallow overburden, quarrying has long been carried out in the area around Portland Bill. Along the East Cliffs, this walk passes former workings, as well as disused cranes that once loaded stone into sea-barges for shipment to Weymouth Harbour.

Portland Lighthouse

Route 12

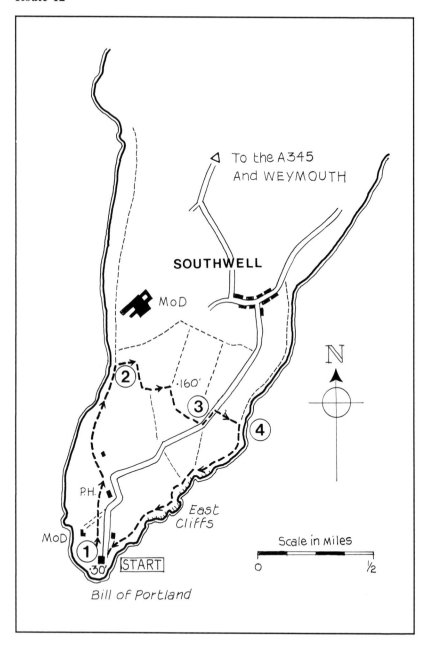

To the A345
And WEYMOUTH

SOUTHWELL

MoD

·160'

N

① ② ③ ④

P.H.

MoD

East Cliffs

① ·30' START

Bill of Portland

Scale in Miles

0   ½

56

Route 12

Around Portland Bill   2½ miles

Start

Follow the A354 southwards from Weymouth to Easton, in the centre of Portland. Beyond Easton, a signposted road leads on to Portland Bill. Park in the public car park at the Bill (fee payable). GR 675683.

Route

1. *Leave the car park at the northern end, furthest away from the lighthouse, cross the MoD base access road and follow the footpath uphill. The path runs to the right of a series of aerials and the coastguard look-out, before passing to the left of the Old Higher Lighthouse. The coast path along the western cliffs of Portland is followed northwards for ¼ mile.*

2. *A short distance before another MoD complex, turn right on to a track indicated by a marker stone. The legend reads 'East Cliffs'. This track follows two sides of a field to a junction, where you continue ahead for 150 yards to a second junction. Turn right, and follow the enclosed path down to the road.*

3. *Turn left, and follow the pavement for a short distance until you reach the second signposted footpath on the opposite side of the road. This path − a gravel track − leads down to a quarry crane on the eastern side of the Isle of Portland.*

4. *Turn right, and follow the coast back to Portland Bill. There are several options − some close to the cliff edge, others rather more inland. Use your discretion! As you approach the Bill, the path passes through a complex of beach huts before bearing right to the car park.*

Refreshments

The Pulpit Inn at Portland Bill lies just a short distance from the car park. There are also several tea shops and snack bars at the Bill.

Public Transport

Southern National operate buses from Weymouth to Portland Bill. Some of these services are operated by open-top vehicles in the summer.

Quarry relics on Portland

The Mohuns of Fleet

Outline
Fleet — The Moonfleet Hotel — The Fleet — East Fleet — Fleet

Summary
Moonfleet is one of the most exciting tales of smugglers and wild seafarers that has ever been written. Generations of youngsters have been thrilled at the adventures of the Mohun Family of Fleet, that remote village on the Dorset coast. This walk follows the sites and sounds of John Meade Faulkner's exciting novel. Along the way lies the church that featured so strongly in Meade's writing, as well as the beach where the *Ebenezer* was wrecked in the 19th century. Be careful on the initial section of road walking — the unclassified lane that is followed does give access to a camp site and can be fairly busy. This part of the walk is soon put behind you, however, as you enjoy the delights of the level coast path beside the Fleet.

Attractions
The low-lying village of Fleet lies just to the east of Chesil Beach. This is a part of the country forever immortalised in John Meade Faulkner's novel *Moonfleet*, that classic tale of smuggling along the Dorset coast. Smuggling was no work of fiction, however. Between 1800 and 1821, 69 men and women from along the Fleet were imprisoned in Dorchester Gaol for handling contraband, chiefly barrels of brandy. A terrific storm in 1824 breached Chesil Beach, and a large part of the original village of Fleet was destroyed. Only the chancel of the old church survives in East Fleet, but it is here that the Mohun Family vault lies beneath the ground . . . but nobody is quite certain where the secret passage leads! A new church was built in the centre of the village in 1829, at the expense of the then vicar, the Reverend John Gould. Sharp eyes will spot a stars-and-stripes in the church. This is to remember the many US troops who were based in Fleet in 1944 prior to the Normandy Landings.

Chesil Beach has been described as 'the eighth wonder of the world'. This pebble beach extends from Portland to Burton Bradstock, with the section between Portland and Abbotsbury enclosing a vast brackish lagoon known as 'The Fleet'. The pebbles along Chesil Beach are finely graded, from the sands of Abbotsbury through to the boulders of Portland. It is even said that fishermen and smugglers in the past could tell whereabouts they had washed up on Chesil under cover of darkness by the size of the pebbles. The Fleet is popular with local fishermen, on account of its fine mullet and bass, whilst bird-watchers will find plenty of interest in and around its waters.

One common species of bird on the Fleet is the mute swan. The swannery at Abbotsbury contains the largest colony of managed swans in the world, and many of these birds find their way along to the section of the Fleet passed on this walk. What attracts so many mute swans to the Fleet is the presence of *Zostera marina*, their

Continued on page 62

Route 13

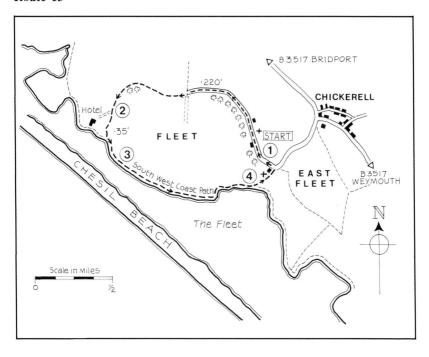

The Mohuns of Fleet   3 miles

Start

Take the B3157 Abbotsbury road out of Weymouth. At Chickerell, just a mile out of the town, turn left on to the unclassified road leading to Fleet. Parking is welcome in the grounds of the new church in exchange for a donation to church funds. GR 634805.

Route

1. *Leave the churchyard and turn right along the lane outside. This lane can be quite busy at times, since it provides access to camp sites and a hotel. In ½ mile, at a crossroads, continue ahead along a driveway leading to Moonfleet Hotel. In another ½ mile, where the drive bears to the right towards the hotel, cross a stile on the left to follow a path signposted to the Coast Path.*

2. *The path crosses a field, the Moonfleet Hotel away to the right. Beyond a stile, the path continues along the edge of a field for just 20 yards to a stile on the right-hand side. Beyond this stile, bear left along the Coast Path signposted to East Fleet and Weymouth.*

3. *Follow the Coast Path for over 1 mile as it borders the Fleet. As you approach East Fleet, the path crosses a stream on a wooden footbridge.*

4. *Do not cross this bridge – rather, turn left away from the coast, along the path signposted to East Fleet and the church. The church lies a short distance ahead, surrounded by fir trees. Follow the path to the right, along the side of the church and in front of a row of cottages out on to the Chickerell to Fleet road. Turn left and, in ¼ mile, you will find yourself back at the 'new' church.*

Refreshments

Meals, drinks and snacks can be obtained at the Moonfleet Hotel. The banks of the Fleet offer many opportunities for picnicking.

Public Transport

Southern National operate Weymouth to Bridport buses that pass through Chickerell, just ½ mile from East Fleet.

Continued from page 59

favourite variety of seaweed. The swans feed by dipping their heads into the water or up-ending to pluck the underwater weeds. The adult male is the largest British bird, weighing upwards of 20 pounds and measuring over 5 feet from the beak to the tail. The body itself is 2 feet in length. To describe the swan as 'mute' is something of a misnomer. The adult birds all too readily snort, hiss or call, whilst the young cygnets are noted for their shrill piping.

Old Church, East Fleet

The Imprint of Ancient Man

Outline
Littlebredy — The Grey Mare and her Colts — Kingston Russell Stone Circle — Foxholes Coppice — Littlebredy

Summary
Littlebredy is an exceptionally picturesque village, lying in a green valley watered by the River Bride. The surrounding hilltops are an archaeologist's dream, being the site of barrows, a stone circle, a 'Celtic' field system and a hut circle. Of particular interest will be *The Grey Mare and her Colts* — a chambered long barrow. A walk that is very much a living history book! This will prove to be one of the more strenuous walks in the book for youngsters, with the fieldpaths and bridleways crossing a hilly section of the Dorset countryside.

Attractions
Littlebredy enjoys a sheltered location deep in the valley of the River Bride. The Bride is a tributary of the River Brit, which flows into the sea at West Bay. The village is made up of a number of thatched cottages and farm buildings, a Victorian church and the stately Bridehead House. A shelter on the village green at the end of the walk will provide a welcome resting spot where the remains of any soft drinks or flasks of coffee can be consumed. The shelter was a gift to the villagers from Philip and Margaret Williams on the occasion of their Silver Wedding in 1933. The Biblical text around the sides of the shelter could almost have been chosen with walkers in mind:
'A pavilion for a shadow in the daytime from the heat and for a
refuge and for a covert from storm and from rain
Isaiah 4v6'
South of Littlebredy lies Tenants Hill, which the OS maps seem to suggest is an open-air museum of archaeology. The hilltop is riddled with tumuli, lynchets, circles and barrows, with three sites being of particular interest.

The Grey Mare and her Colts is today no more than two large standing stones. These were originally part of the main entrance to a chambered long barrow. The pair of megaliths at the eastern end of the barrow would have been crossed by a third stone, forming what archaeologists refer to as a 'trilithon'. The dictionary describes this as 'a monument consisting of three stones, especially of two uprights and a lintel'. This would have been the entrance to a gallery which ran along to an interment at the western end of the Neolithic settlement.

Kingston Russell Stone Circle — also known as the 'Gorwell' circle — dates back as far as 1,500 BC. The 18 stones were originally upright, but the monument has suffered with the passage of time. This is no vast construction, its 80-foot diameter comparing most unfavourably with the famous circles at Stonehenge and Avebury.

Continued on page 66

Route 14

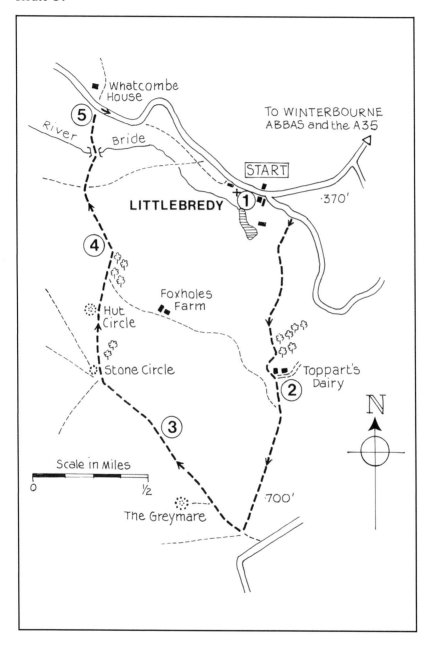

Whatcombe House

River Bride

TO WINTERBOURNE ABBAS and the A35

⑤

START

LITTLEBREDY

①

·370'

④

Foxholes Farm

Hut Circle

Stone Circle

Toppart's Dairy

②

③

Scale in Miles

0   ½

The Greymare

·700'

N

Route 14

The Imprint of Ancient Man   4½ miles

Start

Follow the A35 westwards out of Dorchester for 5 miles to Winterborne Abbas. Just to the west of the village, turn on to the unclassified road signposted to Littlebredy. Park in the vicinity of the village church. GR 588890.

Route

1. *With your back to the church, walk to the right along the road to a junction. Turn right and, in 300 yards, right again on to a bridlepath that borders the village cricket pitch. Pass through a gateway at the far side of the field, and continue following the path uphill through a clump of trees. The bridlepath continues across the hillside and alongside Farm Wood, to reach a gateway beside Toppart's Dairy.*

2. *Beyond the gateway, turn right on to the driveway that leads away from Toppart's Dairy. In ¾ mile at a junction, turn right through a gateway to follow a path signposted to Kingston Russell Stone Circle. Follow the left-hand hedgerows across 3 hilltop fields.*
   NB: A detour is necessary to find 'The Grey Mare and her Colts'. Just as you enter the second field, cross a stile on the left. Follow the left-hand hedgerow for 150 yards to a gateway, the other side of which you will find the long barrow.

3. *At the far side of the third field, pass through a handgate on the left-hand side. Bear half right across the next field, passing the stone circle, to reach a gateway in the fence, with the Bride Valley lying ahead. Head across to the obvious hut circle, and descend the hillside beyond, bearing to the left all the time to reach the woodland at the foot of the slope. Continue along the edge of the field at the bottom of the slope to another gateway.*

4. *Pass through this gate, and turn left to follow the hedgerow for 100 yards. At this point, bear right to a gate at the bottom of the field. Cross to another gateway at the far side of the next field, beyond which the path crosses the River Bride before passing through a gate and following the field boundary ahead to a road.*

5. *Across the road lies Whatcombe House. Turn right, and follow what is a quiet lane the ¾ mile back into Littlebredy. Along the way, there are fine views back to the right of the hillsides you have just negotiated.*

Refreshments

There are no refreshment facilities on this walk. The best option is to pack a picnic, which can be enjoyed in the vicinity of Littlebredy Church.

Continued from page 63

Purists, however, will prefer the Kingston Russell Circle, high on a hilltop and over a mile from the nearest road access. As with so many ancient monuments, its function remains something of a mystery. Obviously, the circle had some religious function, but what this was is a matter of some debate.

The hut circles to the north of the Kingston Russell Stone Circle sit on the edge of the hilltop, enjoying a spectacular view across the Bride Valley. This would have been an excellent defensive location in centuries past, with any unwelcome visitors being visible from far off. The hut circles are all that remain of the homes of the ancient settlers in this part of the Dorset Downs. The raised embankments represent the foundations of a series of circular huts, constructed quite simply of earth. To keep the family dry, a roof of branches would have decked out the homestead. It may have been crude and rudimentary, but these huts would have provided welcome shelter on what is an open and exposed hilltop site.

Public Transport

This is an isolated corner of Dorset with no public transport facilities.

The Grey Mare and her Colts

66

Powerstock and Eggardon Hill

Outline
Powerstock − Nettlecombe − North Eggardon Farm − Eggardon Hill − Powerstock

Summary
Venture away from the coast in West Dorset and you will find a countryside characterised by rolling hills, deep valleys and isolated village communities. This is all too evident as you drive eastwards from Bridport along the narrow, winding lanes that lead to Powerstock! This walk explores this traditional rural landscape, following quiet lanes and deserted bridlepaths that lead from Powerstock to Eggardon Hill. The hilltop is the spectacular location of an Iron Age hill fort. A relatively long excursion that involves a steep climb on to Eggardon Hill, but the reward for your efforts is a truly memorable day out on the Dorset hills.

Attractions
Powerstock genuinely deserves to be labelled as one of the most attractive villages in Dorset. Picture-postcard stone and thatch cottages lie scattered across steep hillsides, above a tributary stream of the River Brit. The stone church sits imposingly upon its own knoll, as if keeping a watchful eye on the moral and spiritual conduct of the parishioners! The church was restored in the mid-19th century, although the Norman chancel arch and the 15th century south doorway hark back to an earlier era. Along the road from the church lies the Three Horseshoes Inn, fully deserving its entry in *The Good Pub Guide*. This hostelry is well known for its fish dishes, which could be accompanied by a pint of Palmer's Best, a fine beer brewed locally in Bridport. Behind the inn is a sloping garden, with delightful views across Powerstock and the nearby hillsides.

Eggardon Hill is the site of one of the finest hill forts in Wessex (the author's own personal favourite). This Iron Age settlement sits high on a ridge of the Dorset Downs, with commanding views that stretch both inland and far out to sea. It is a bi-vallate construction, designed for slingstone warfare. This is evident from the distance between the inner and outer ramparts. As you explore this hilltop site, scrutinise the ground carefully and you may well find the odd slingstone. The ramparts enclose a site of some 20 acres, where archaeologists have unearthed 120 depressions − the sites of Stone Age homes. Walls of earth and a roof of branches would have provided welcome shelter on this windswept and exposed hilltop.

The careful eye will spot a couple of old railway bridges and a residence called *The Old Station* on the fringes of Powerstock. These are the remains of what must have been one of England's most scenic railways − the Bridport Branch. The line was opened in 1857, and was originally a broad gauge track running from the GWR line at Maiden Newton. This was one of five seaside branch lines in the county, all of

Continued on page 70

Route 15

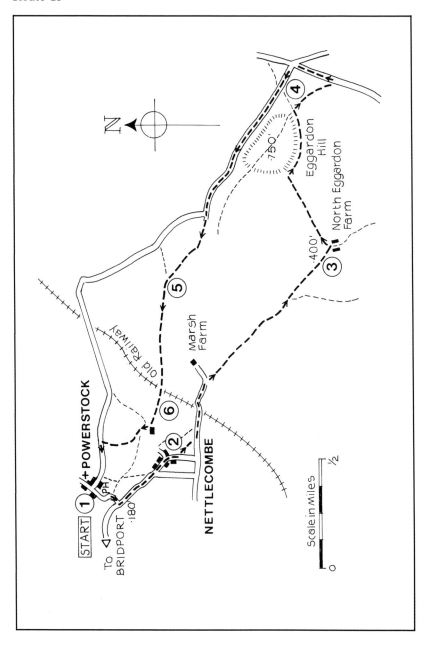

Route 15

Powerstock and Eggardon Hill   **5 miles**

Start

Leave the A3066 Bridport to Beaminster road at Gore Cross, just a mile out of Bridport, and follow the unclassified road that is signposted to Powerstock. In the centre of the village, turn right at the church along the Whetley and Eggardon Hill turning. Park carefully on this road somewhere between the church and the Three Horseshoes Inn. GR 516962.

Route

1. Return to the crossroads by the church, and turn left along the road that leads back to Bridport. In 400 yards, at a junction, turn left along the lane that leads to Nettlecombe. In another 400 yards, follow the lane in front of the Marquis of Lorne Inn, which continues through Nettlecombe.

2. Just on the edge of the village, cross a stone-slab stile on the left-hand side and walk across to the far right-hand corner of what is the local cricket ground. Beyond a gate, turn left along a lane which is followed for over 1 mile to North Eggardon Farm. This lane passes The Old Station and a turning to Marsh Farm before it becomes an unmetalled bridlepath.

3. Alongside the farm buildings, turn left on to a bridleway signposted to Eggardon Hill. The obvious path climbs the hillside for almost ½ mile, before entering an enclosure with the hill fort's ramparts directly ahead. Turn right, and follow the ditch between the ramparts for 600 yards to a stile and an NT sign − detours to explore this magnificent hilltop site are almost obligatory!

4. Cross the stile and, in just a few yards, pass through a handgate on the left. Cross to a second handgate on the far side of the field. Turn left beyond this gate, and follow a hilltop lane back towards Powerstock. In ½ mile, where this lane bears right, turn left on to a path signposted to Powerstock.

5. This path soon enters open countryside, where it continues as a well-defined track across 2 fields. Beyond the second field, it reverts to being an enclosed track. In a short distance, leave the track at a stile to follow a footpath on the right signposted to Powerstock. This path very soon follows the right-hand edge of a field down to a stile and a bridge across the old railway.

6. Continue down the edge of the field beyond the railway to a stile on the right, just past a gateway. Beyond this stile, the path descends through damp, shady woodland to Castle Mill Farm. Turn right by the thatched cottage along the bridlepath signposted to Powerstock. This path joins the Eggardon Lane in just

¼ mile. Turn left, and in another ¼ mile you will be back at the Three Horseshoes and the church.

Refreshments
At journey's end, the Three Horseshoes Inn provides excellent food and drink, as well as a welcoming garden. Eggardon Hill would make for an excellent picnic stop.

Public Transport
Mike Halford operates a bus service between Bridport and Maiden Newton that passes through Powerstock.

Looking North from Eggardon Hill

Continued from page 67
which fell victim to competition from the roads. The other seaside lines ran to Swanage, Portland, Abbotsbury and Lyme Regis. With the Bridport Branch finally closing in 1975, visitors to Dorset wishing to sample the delights of a seaside railway will have to visit Swanage. The Swanage Branch is in the process of being restored by a group of steam enthusiasts.

Ramparts on Eggardon Hill

The Three Horseshoes, Powerstock

71

High on Golden Cap

Outline
Seatown − Langdon Hill − Golden Cap − Seatown

Summary

A short climb out of the coastal resort of Seatown brings you on to the Golden Cap. At 626 feet above sea level, this is the highest cliff in Southern England. Needless to say, the views are quite superb − a clear day is a must on this particular excursion. By way of compensation, the return leg of the walk follows a downhill section of the Dorset Coast Path.

Attractions

Seatown lies at the end of a narrow lane, a mile or so south of Chideock on the busy A35. Either side of the shingle beach lies some of Dorset's loveliest coastline, Ridge Cliff to the east and Wear Cliffs to the west. It comes as no surprise to discover that this lonely and isolated section of the coast was populated by smugglers in centuries past. Many a keg of brandy would have been landed at Seatown under cover of darkness, with the local network of tracks and lanes being used to distribute the contraband to nearby villages. Today, the village is an altogether more peaceful place. Thatched cottages, fashioned from honey-coloured stone, line the main street, which ends on the coast alongside the 18th century Anchor Inn. Beyond the inn lies the shingle beach, where shore-fishing for bass and mackerel is an especially popular pastime.

The Golden Cap, at 626 feet above sea level, is the highest cliff in Southern England. The name comes from the coloration of the cliff's summit, where golden sandstone and clumps of gorse bushes reflect a golden hue in bright sunlight. The Golden Cap itself is simply the centrepiece of a 2,000 acre estate owned and managed by the National Trust. The property consists of hill, farmland, cliff, undercliff and beach between Charmouth and Eypemouth. From the flat summit of Golden Cap, the views are exceptional. Be sure to walk beyond the trig point to the western end of the summit, a superb vantage point across Lyme Bay.

The return to Seatown follows the Dorset Coast Path, itself an integral part of the South-West Peninsula Coast Path. Running from Minehead in Somerset to Poole Harbour in Dorset, this 515 mile path is the longest long-distance path in Great Britain. It is actually twice as long as its nearest rival, the Pennine Way. *500 Mile Walkies* (Arrow Books) is Mark Wallington's humorous account of walking the South-West Peninsula Coast Path with his dog Boogie. He describes the climb on to the

Golden Cap with typical wit:

> 'Golden Cap could be conquered with the right tactics. Walk a few yards, stop, have a drink, a hunk of chocolate and a little lie down, then walk another few yards. An hour and whole bar of Galaxy later, I finally scrambled up to the summit.'

Seatown

Route 16

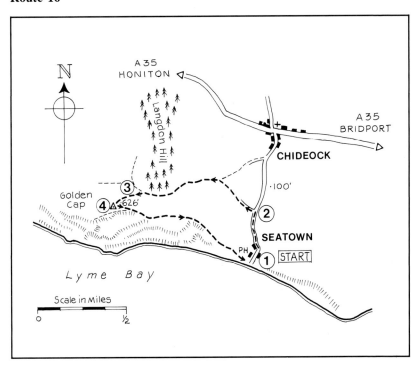

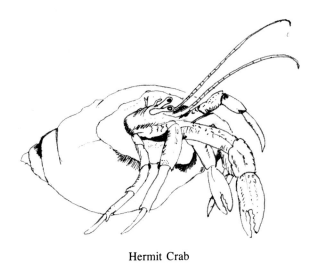

Hermit Crab

74

Route 16

High on Golden Cap   2 miles

Start
From Chideock, 4 miles west of Bridport on the A35 trunk road to Honiton, follow the signposted lane southwards to Seatown. There is a car park alongside the beach (fee payable). GR 421918.

Route
1. *Leave the car park and turn right along the lane heading back towards Chideock. In 400 yards, turn left on to a track signposted to Langdon Hill. A small bench sits at the junction.*

2. *Follow this enclosed track uphill towards the woodland at the top of Langdon Hill, ignoring any right turns. Just before the hilltop, the path passes through a gateway and continues around the southern edge of the woodland.*

3. *Where the woodland ends, follow the path ahead signposted to Golden Cap. This path follows a clearly visible route, crossing a stile and passing through a kissing-gate, before climbing to what is the highest point on the south coast of England.*

4. *Having explored the area around Golden Cap, retrace your steps back downhill to the kissing-gate. Rather than continuing back to Langdon Hill, turn right on to the signposted Coast Path. The path is well defined and follows an obvious route back to Seatown, clearly visible several hundred feet below. As you enter the village, turn left in front of the Anchor Inn to return to the car park.*

Refreshments
The Anchor Inn in Seatown serves a good range of beers and bar meals, as well as cream teas.

Public Transport
Bridport to Lyme Regis buses, run by Southern National, pass through Chideock. This village is only ½ mile from point 2 on the walk.

Seatown Beach

Useful information

Routes in order of difficulty

As an experienced walker, I would class all of the walks in this book as relatively easy if I were tackling them on my own. However, these are Family Walks and the grading should be read with this in mind. They apply to a fairly active eight or nine year old, rather than a hardened veteran of the hills!

Very easy walks:
Route   3 − Badbury Rings − 3 miles
Route   4 − Arne and Arne Heath − 2½ miles
Route 12 − Around Portland Bill − 2½ miles
Route 13 − The Mohuns of Fleet − 3 miles

Easy walks with a short climb:
Route   2 − Hod Hill − 3 miles
Route   7 − Lulworth Cove and Durdle Door − 2 miles
Route 10 − The Cerne Abbas Giant − 2½ miles
Route 11 − Maiden Castle − 2½ miles
Route 16 − High on Golden Cap − 2 miles

More difficult:
Route   1 − Cranborne Chase − 4 miles
Route   5 − Studland and Old Harry − 4 miles
Route   9 − Puddletown Forest and Hardy's Cottage − 4 miles

Difficult:
Route   6 − St Aldhelm's Head − 5 miles
Route   8 − Tolpuddle and Weatherby Castle − 5 miles
Route 14 − The Imprint of Ancient Man − 4½ miles
Route 15 − Powerstock and Eggardon Hill − 5 miles

Bus operators in the area

Dorset County Council publish a leaflet entitled 'Bus and Rail Map for Rural Dorset', which gives a comprehensive listing of all public transport operators in the county. The companies listed below are the ones whose services coincide with the walks in this book.
Mike Halford Tel. (01308) 421106
Southern National Tel. (01305) 783645
Wiltshire & Dorset Tel. (01202) 673555
Garrison Cars Tel. (01929) 462467

Tourist information centres in the area

Blandford Forum. Ham Car Park, Tel. (01258) 51989
Bournemouth. Westover Road. Tel. (01202) 291715
Bridport. 32 South Street. Tel. (01308) 24901
Christchurch. Saxon Square. Tel. (01202) 471780
Dorchester. 7 Acland Road. Tel. (0305) 67992
Lyme Regis. The Guildhall. Tel. (01297) 442138
Poole. The Quay. Tel. (01202) 673322
Portland. St George's Centre. Tel. (01305) 823406
Shaftesbury. County Library. Tel. (01747) 853514
Sherborne. Hound Street. Tel. (01935) 815341
Swanage. The White House, Shore Road. Tel. (01929) 422885

Wareham. Town Hall. Tel. (01929) 552740
Weymouth. The Esplanade. Tel. (01305) 785747
Wimborne. Cook Row. Tel. (0202) 886116

Wet weather alternatives

A selection of attractions completely or partly under cover.

Museums

Arne − A World of Toys. Toys and musical box museum. Open daily April-September (closed Mondays and Saturdays except August).

Blandford Forum Museum. Local history and rural memorabilia. Open daily April-September except Sundays.

Bridport Museum. Local history. Open daily Easter-October, open Wednesdays, Saturdays and Sundays November-Easter.

Corfe Castle Museum. Local history. Open daily.

Dorchester − County Museum. Local history, geology, archaeology, Maiden Castle, Thomas Hardy, etc. Open Monday-Saturday.

Lulworth Cove Museum. Geological displays. Open daily except Mondays and Fridays.

Lyme Regis Museum. Geology, archaeology, local history. Open daily.

Portland Museum. Fascinating local displays. Open daily Easter-October, closed Mondays November-Easter.

Shaftesbury Museum. Local history displays. Open daily Easter-September.

Sherborne Museum. History of the town. Open Easter-October except Mondays.

Swanage Museum. Local displays housed in tithe barn. Open daily May-September.

Tolpuddle Martyrs' Museum. Housed in the TUC Memorial Cottages in Tolpuddle. Open daily except Mondays.

Wareham Town Museum. Local history and archaeology. Open Easter-October except Sundays.

West Bay Harbour Museum. Local fishing exhibits. Open daily April-September.

Weymouth Deep Sea Centre. Nautical displays. Open daily.

Historic buildings

Abbotsbury Tithe Barn Country Museum. Open daily Easter-October.

Clouds Hill Cottage. Home of Lawrence of Arabia. Check opening times with Dorchester TIC.

Corfe Castle. Imposing ruin. Open daily March-October.

Dorchester Old Crown Court. Scene of Tolpuddle Martyrs' Trial. Open Monday-Friday.

Hardy's Cottage. Thomas Hardy's birthplace. Open by appointment with custodian.

Kingston Lacy Estate. Vast National Trust property. Open April-October except Thursdays and Fridays.

Portland Castle. One of Henry VIII's castles. Open summer months.

Portland Lighthouse. Open as advertised locally.

Shaftesbury Abbey. Remains of Benedictine nunnery. Open daily Good Friday-October.

Sherborne Abbey. Imposing church, the former seat of the Saxon Bishop of Wessex. Open daily.

Sherborne Castle. Built by Sir Walter Raleigh in 1594. Open Easter-September Thursdays, Saturdays, Sundays and Bank Holiday Mondays.

Wimborne Minster. Imposing church of mixed architectural styles, ranging from Transitional to Perpendicular. Open daily.

Other places of interest

Bovington Camp. 250 tanks on display. Open daily.
Dorchester Dinosaur Centre. Open daily.
Lyme Regis Aquarium. On the Cobb. Open daily May-September.
Monkey World – Wool. Open daily.
Morecombelake – Moores' Biscuit Factory. Family factory 112 years old. Open Monday-Friday.
Poole Pottery. Showroom and craft centre. Open Monday-Saturday.
Swanage Railway. Open daily June-September and weekends.
Weymouth Sealife Experience. Displays of marine life. Open daily.
Wimborne – William Walker Glass. Hand-made glassware. Open Monday-Saturday.

This is of necessity only a selection of the attractions in Dorset. Visitors are strongly advised to invest in a copy of *The Golden Eye Map-Guide to Dorset*, which provides a comprehensive listing of the county's rich and varied attractions.

The view to Durdle Moor

THE FAMILY WALKS SERIES

The publishers welcome suggestions for future titles and will be pleased to consider manuscripts relating to Derbyshire from new and established authors.

Scarthin Books of Cromford, in the Peak District, are also leading new, second-hand and antiquarian booksellers, and are eager to purchase specialised material, both ancient and modern. Contact Dr. D.J. Mitchell 01629 823272.